ISBN - 9781479229260

Table of Contents

A Quick Word on Referencing Reference Materials

This book is intended to provide a step-by-step method for formatting your paper for MLA. The nature of this book is somewhat tenuous because it is a quick manual for a particular method of writing papers that has been established by writers – in other words, the information has already been written down by known authorities on the subject. With that said, let it be known that while there are other formatting methods (APA, Turabian, Chicago, etc.) this quick MLA guide finds its roots in the MLA Handbook for Writers of Research Papers, Seventh Edition (the most recent edition). If you are dealing with more nuanced MLA issues, I recommend checking out the aforementioned book from your local library. Over the years, I have come to know MLA and Turrabian like I know "the back of my hand," so all references in those chapters listed above are my own thoughts taken from this book or previous editions of that MLA book and simplified for your ease of use.

MLA and Microsoft Word Menu

Microsoft Word is a great word processing program to use. New to the fourth edition is MSWORD (2010) for Windows. However, Microsoft Word 2008 and 2011 (for Mac) are still used in this book. There is one item mentioned for the purposes of our discussion that may seem confusing: When I refer to Menu throughout the book I am referring to the images listed below – this is the Menu bar (the first one is for MSWORD for Windows, the second one is for MSWORD for Mac):

Menu for MSWORD For Windows

Menu for MSWORD For MAC

MLA and Pages by Apple Menu

Pages is a great word processing program to use. Just like MSWord, I have found that little changes with Pages over the years. As with the MSWORD program listed above, there are three items mentioned for the purposes of our discussion that may seem confusing: First, when I refer to **Menu** throughout the book I am referring to the image listed below – this is the **Menu** bar:

Second, when I refer to the **Inspector Menu**, I am referring to the image below (In particular the little images at the top of the picture (a dog-eared white piece of paper, the columns, the T, the little ruler, the Q, etc.:

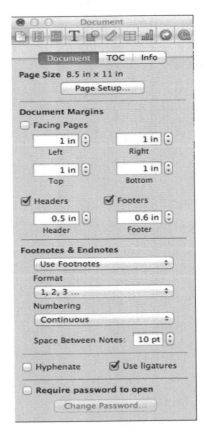

Personally, I really like using the **Inspector Menu**. I find it very intuitive and easy to manage. To see or show your Inspector Menu (sometimes it is hidden), you can do one of two things. You can locate the button on the top of your paper that looks like (Image - 0) shown below:

Or you can use the **Menu** to show your **Inspector Menu**: Go to **View → Show Inspector** as shown in (Image 0.1).

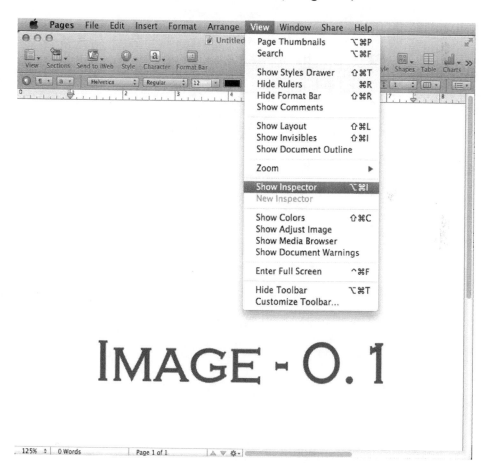

Third, one other thing that you should know is that if you see an → symbol, it is informing you of some steps to take such as **Menu→Inspector Menu→Document Inspector**. I have included a number of photos which will also guide you through the process in case you are a more visual learner. In this case you will want to follow the Red Circles. I have some circles in Blue which are to help you make sure that you are in the right place in case you are confused. However, the Red circles are intended to help you know what you need to push and edit, etc. For those of you who purchased the paperback version, I shall make note throughout the book as to which circles you are to be aware of.

Chapter 1: Paper Formatting For MSWORD 2010 (Windows)

1. Paper Set-Up: Margins

1. With your Page open up to a blank page find the **Page Layout** button in the **Menu**. (see MSW-1).

2. Click on **Page Layout** (see MSW-1).
3. On the left-hand side find the **Margins** box (see MSW-2) under the section of Page Setup.

4. Click on **Margins** (see MSW-2).
5. It brings down a Drop-down box where you have several selections. You want to make sure that your selection is **Normal**. Click on **Normal (**see MSW-2.1).

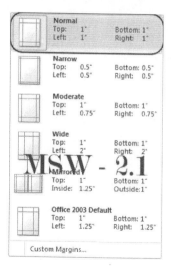

Normal is 1" settings all the way around the paper – this is MLA standard.

    a. An alternate step is to click on Custom Margins (at the bottom of the drop down menu). After you click on **Custom Margins** it opens a window where you can adjust everything under the heading of Page Setup.

6. Congratulations! You have just setup your margins for your MLA paper!

2. Paper Set-Up: Header and Footer (Last Name and Page Number)

1. Go to your **Menu** and click on the **Insert** button (see MSW-3).

2. Towards the Middle on the Right-hand side there is a section called Header & Footer. You want to click on **Header** (see MSW-4).

3. This will bring down a drop-down menu of choices. You want to click on the first one that says **Blank** (see MSW-4.1).

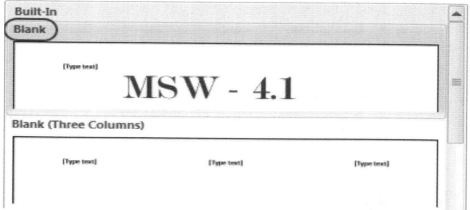

4. You will now see that your paper has inserted a header onto the top of your page (see MSW-5).

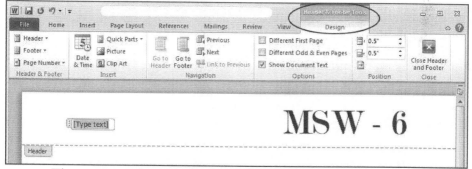

And you should now see that the Menu now lists a **Header Design Page** (see MSW-6).

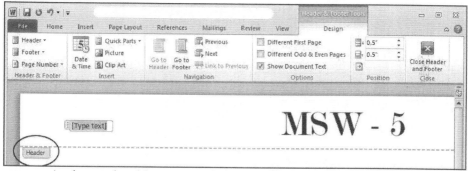

The next step is to move the typing to the Right-hand side of the page (It should have shown up on the left hand side of the page – if you look at MSW-5 and MSW-6 you will see that there is an area

at the top of the page where there is a box that says [Type text].)
You will need to **Right** align the typing.

5. On the right-hand side of the Header Design tab, you will see a
   section that says Position (see MSW-7). Above the word Position,
   you will see a little box with an arrow in it (see MSW-7). Click on
   this **Little Arrowed Box**.

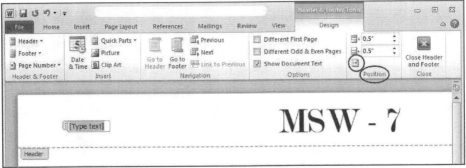

6. This opened up a new window entitled Alignment Tab (see MSW-
   8). Underneath alignment tab you will see three selections Left,
   Center, Right. You want to check the **Right** button.

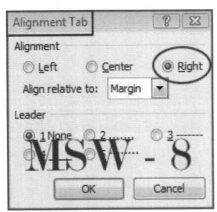

7. Click **OK**.
8. Great! You have just aligned your typing to the right hand side of
   your footer, which is exactly where it needs to be for MLA
   formatting for Last Name and Number on each paper.

3. Formatting the Page Number

1. Let's do the Page Number First! On the left-hand side of the Header Design Page, you will see a selection that says Header and Footer (see MSW-9). Within this Header and Footer section there is a button that says **Page Number**. Click on **Page Number** (see MSW-9).

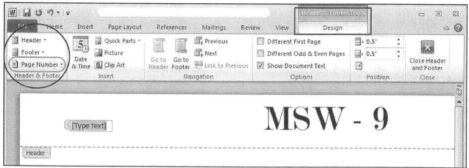

2. It will bring a drop down menu where you will need to choose **Top of Page**. Click on **Top of Page**.

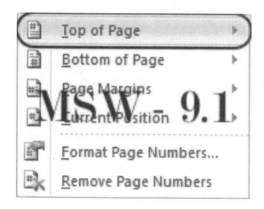

3. This will bring up another drop down menu where you will choose the selection **Plain Number 3**. Click on **Plain Number 3**.

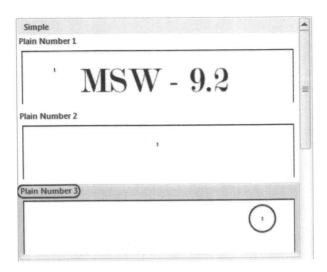

4. You should now see a number 1 at the top right-hand corner of your page. Next, type your Last Name. After you finish typing your last name be sure to give a few spaces between your last name and the number.

5. You will see that your Paper should look like image MSW-10.

6. You can now close the Header and Footer. To close the Header and Footer, click on the big red X on the right-hand side of the page that says "**Close Header and Footer**" (see MSW-10). (if you need to change something in the Header, just click on your last name or somewhere within the Header and it will open up the Header again).

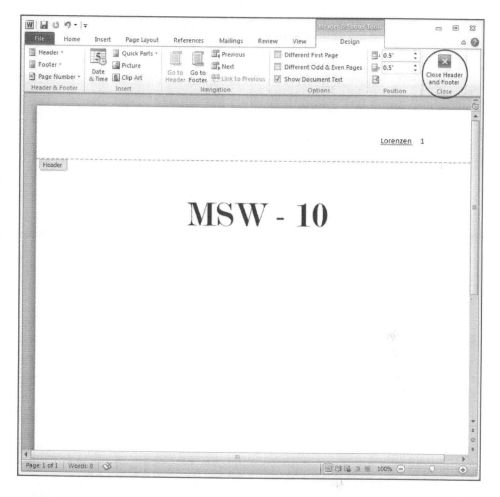

4. Page Set-Up: Name, Professor, Course, Course Number, and Date

1. You now need to Double Space your paper. Go to your **Menu** and Click on the **Home** button.
2. In the Middle of the Home Menu you will see a section that says **Paragraph**. On the right hand side of the **Paragraph** section there is a button that has an arrow going up and an arrow going down. Click on this button (see MSW-11).

15

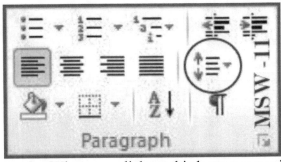

3. When you click on this button you will see several choices of how you want to space the lines in your paper. Click the one that says **2.0**. (see MSW 11.1)

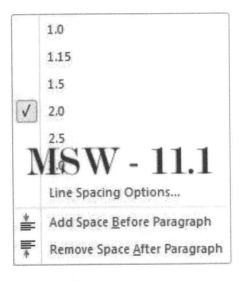

1.0

1.15

1.5

✓ 2.0

2.5

MSW - 11.1

Line Spacing Options...

Add Space Before Paragraph

Remove Space After Paragraph

4. Great job! Your whole paper will now be double-spaced which is exactly where it needs to be for MLA format!

5. Starting from the Left hand side of your paper (if your cursor isn't on the left hand side of the paper) go to **Home →Paragraph→ Align Text Left** (see MSW-12)) type Your Name - hit the enter or return(on the keyboard); **type your Professor's Name** - hit enter or return(on the keyboard); **type your Course Name and Number** - hit enter or return(on the keyboard); **type the Date** - hit enter or return (on the keyboard).

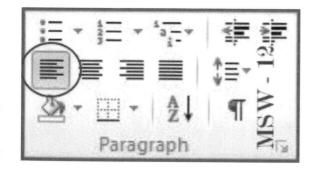

If you need to look at an example of what your paper should look like at this point, take a look at image MSW-14.

5. Page Set-Up: Title of your Paper

1. You just finished typing the Name, Professor, Course, Course Number, and Date. The Next Step is to place your title on your paper. You will want to start by **Centering your Title** in the middle of your paper. To do so go to your **Home Menu** (you should already be here if you just finished following the instructions above).
2. Find the **Paragraph** section. And click on the button for **Center** (see MSW-13).

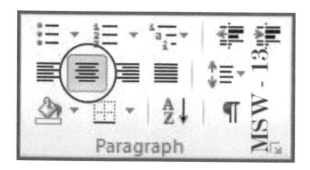

3. Great! You are now ready to type in the title of your paper! **Type your title!**
4. When you finish typing your title, **hit enter or return** (on the keyboard).

*** Three Additional Notes When Titling Your Paper***

There are three things you want to keep in mind when you **Title** your paper. **First, you want to capitalize the start of every word in your Title with the exception of: articles** (a, an, the), prepositions (of, in, around, about, etc.), or coordinating conjunctions (for, and, nor, but, yet, so). The exception to this rule is that you do want to capitalize the first letter of the start of your Title, no matter of what it is. So, if the start of your Title begins with The, you want to capitalize the T (see MSW-14).

Second, do not capitalize a whole word or all of the words in your Title (see MSW-14).

Third, you never underline your Title, but should you reference a longer/larger work *within* your Title, you need to italicize the book, magazine, or a longer/larger work. If you are referencing a relatively short work like an article for a newspaper or magazine or a poem then you will want to use quotation marks around the referenced work – just like you would in the body of your paper. If you take a look at Image – P you will see that I created a Title with a reference to a book within the Title. Notice how the book Title within the paper Title is italicized (see MSW-14).

6. Page Set-Up: Formatting the Intro, Body, and Conclusion

1. If you just finished typing the title on your paper and you hit enter or return on your keyboard, you will notice that the cursor is still in the middle of the page. We need to align that cursor to the left-hand side of the page. To do so go to **Home** Menu (again, you should already be here). Find the **Paragraph** section in the middle of the Home Menu. Click on the **Left Align** button (see MSW-12).

You are now ready to start typing your paper!

Chapter 2 – Formatting Your Paper for MSWORD (for MAC/Apple)

Starting Your Paper (MS WORD for MAC/Apple):

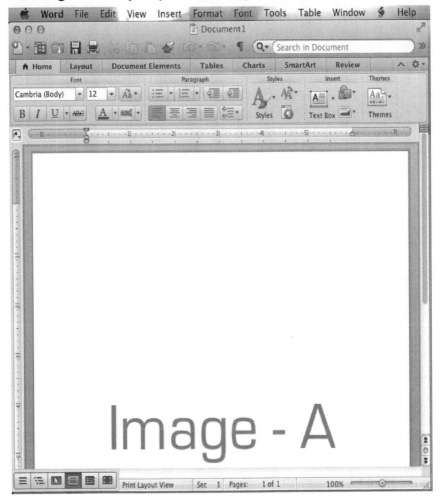

1. Paper Set-Up: Margins (MSWORD for MAC/Apple)

Whether you have already completed your work or you are just starting, these steps will be exactly the same.

1. Go to the top of your Menu where it says: **File** and click on **File**. It will drop down a menu to choose from.

2. You will want to choose **Page Setup** (See Image – B).

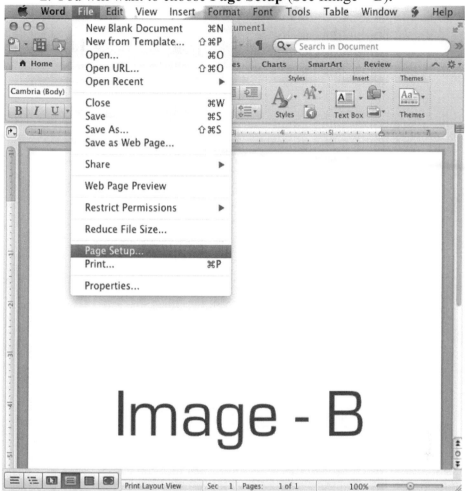

Image - B

MAC USERS, ONLY: For Mac users there are a couple of extra steps involved. Once you choose Page Setup it will open a window that looks like Image – C. When the window appears it will default to **Page Attributes**. You want to click on **Page Attributes** and select or click on **Microsoft Word** (See Image – C).

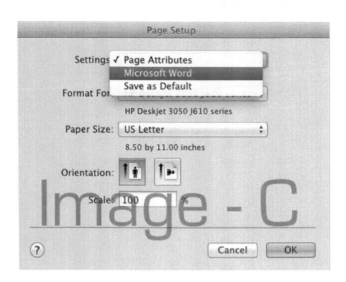

This will bring you to another window, pictured in Image – D. If you see where it says **Margins…** you want to click on the **Margins…** button (See Image – D).

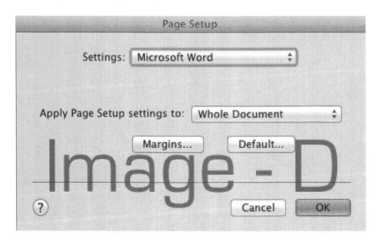

3. You will now see a screen that looks something like the picture on (Image—E). The default selection is one inch (1") margins on the top and on the bottom, but an inch and a quarter (1¼" or 1.25) for the left and the right. MLA guidelines state that the margins on all sides must be one inch (1"). This means that you will need to change the margins on the Left and Right to read (1").

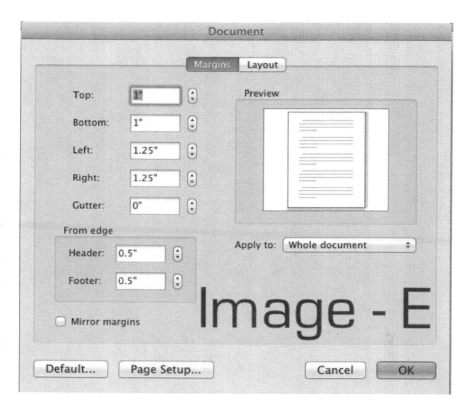

4. When you are finished typing in 1" margins on all sides your window should look something like the picture on (Image – F). You are now ready to click "**OK**" – this will create your 1" margins.

5. Click "**OK**"

Congratulations! You have just set up the margins for your paper. Good work!

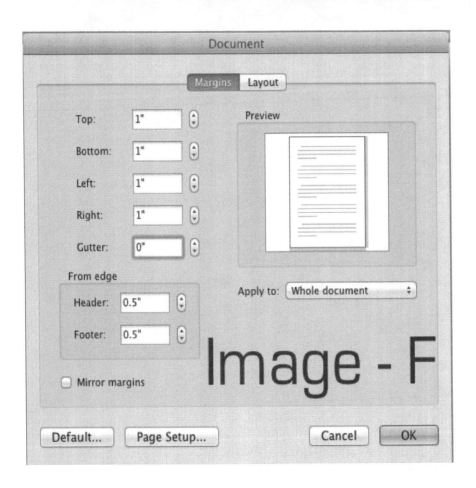

2. *Paper Set-Up: Header and Footer (Last Name and Page Number) (MSWORD for MAC/Apple)*

Depending on how you have your Microsoft Word program formatted, you may have the header and footer showing whenever you open up a new document. For those of you that don't have your header and footer defaulted to show up automatically, this next step will show you how to "show" your header and footer.

1. Go to the top of your Menu where it says **View** and click on **View**.

2. It will bring up a list of many different choices – one of which is **Header and Footer**. You want to select **Header and Footer** (See Image – G).

Unless you are instructed to do so by your professor, MLA guidelines do not demand a title page which means that it is best not to have one (unless you are told to do so – always check with your professor).

3. Now that you have your Header and Footer (see Image – H), you are ready to enter your name into the upper right hand corner of the paper in the **Header**.

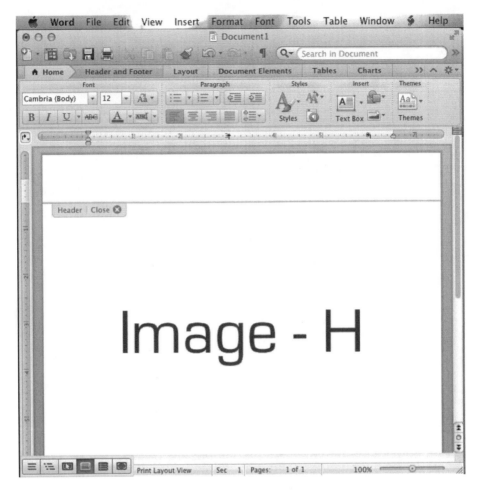

4. Microsoft Word will always default so that your typing starts from the Left. In this case you want your typing to start from the Right. This will take a couple of steps.

5. Go to the top of your Menu where it says **Format**. Click on **Format** and it will bring up a number of choices. You will want to click on the one that says **Paragraph** (see Image – I).

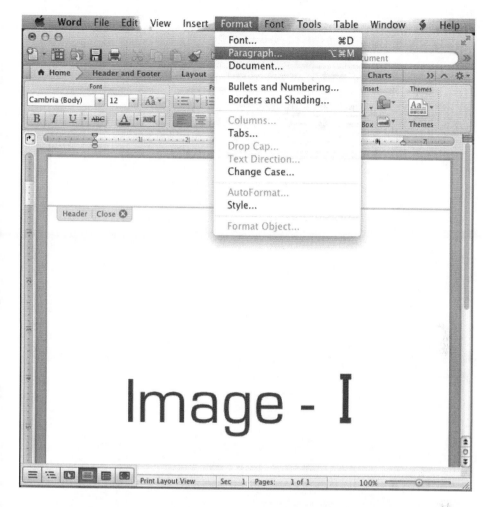

6. Now that you have clicked on **Paragraph** it opened up a new window where you can set the **Alignment** of your cursor.

7. Click on the **Left** button and it will open up a drop down menu where you can now adjust the alignment of the cursor to start on the **Right** side of the paper (see Image – J) (remember you are still in the Header, so it will only make the adjustment to the Header, not the rest of your paper. If you ever need to make the same Alignment changes in your paper follow the same steps within the body of your paper).

8. Now that you have selected the **Right**, click **OK**. Your alignment is now on the right hand side – Good work!

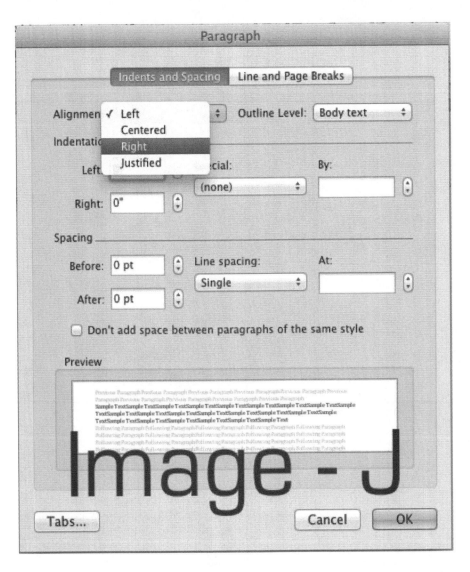

If you look back to the **Margins** section of this manual, you will see that the Margins for the **Header and Footer** default to **.50** or ½ inch. This is exactly where they need to be for MLA guidelines. If you find that they are off, just follow the instructions in the **Margins** section and set the Margins to .50. Also, always remember that your *Last name* and *page number* are flush against the Right side of the paper. When it is finished your paper should look something like (Image – K). **Notice the last name followed by a space followed by the number 1, indicating that it is the first page of the paper.** You want to make sure that each additional page of the paper looks like this - except changing the number as the pages continue.

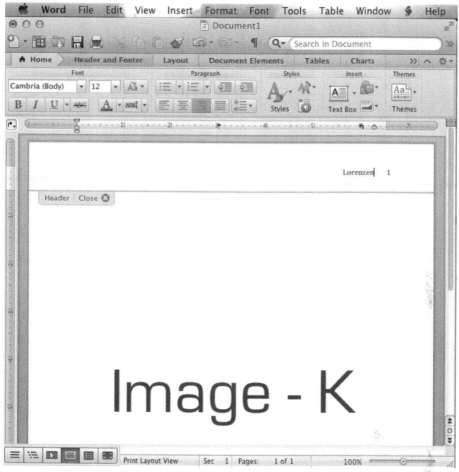

3. ***Inserting the Number*** (MSWORD for MAC/Apple)

An additional note to consider is that you can't just put in the number 1 after your name – Word won't recognize that you are going to be counting pages after this first page.

1. So, in order to have Word recognize that you are going to be counting pages after this page go back to your **Menu** and choose **Insert**.

2. It will bring down a drop menu where you will want to choose **Page Numbers** (see Image – L). You will notice that a page number appeared in the Header (hopefully after your name, assuming that you haven't clicked your cursor somewhere else).

3. Now Word will recognize each subsequent page as an additional page to your paper. After you have finished entering in your name and inserted the page number after this you can go ahead and **Close** the **Header and Footer** (If you see Images – K and L, you see that there is a Close with an X after it. Click that X and it will close the Header and Footer. If ever you need to get back to the Header and Footer just follow the instructions I gave earlier and it will allow you to access the Header and Footer. Good work with your Header and Footer!

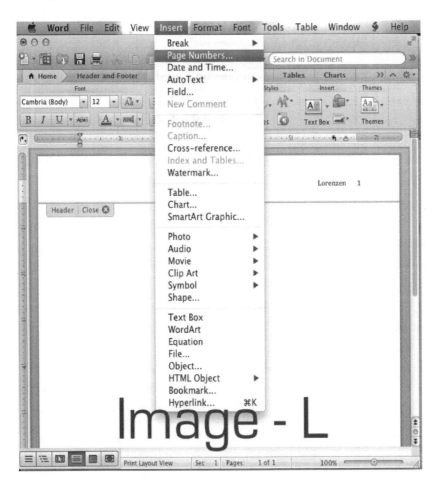

4. Paper Set-Up: Name, Professor, Course and Course Number, and Date (MSWORD for MAC/Apple)

You are now ready to place your name, your professor's name, the course name and number, and date on your paper.

1. Starting from the top left hand side of the body of your paper, place **your full name and double space; place your professors name and double space; place your course name and number and double space; and place the date and double space**.

When you are finished your paper should look something like the picture in image (M).

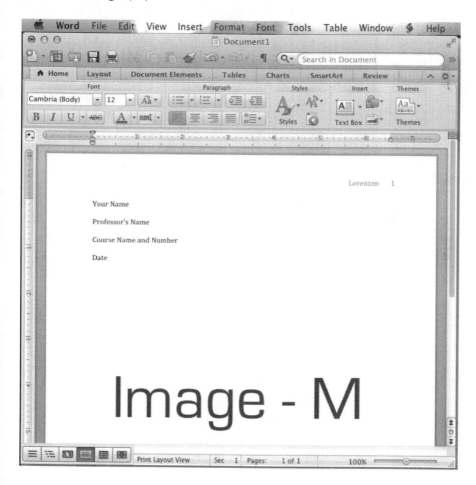

5. Page Set-Up: Title of Paper (MSWORD for MAC/Apple)

The next step is to place your title on your paper. You have just finished placing the date on your paper – you now want to double space after the date.

1. If you remember back to the **Alignment** of the Header and Footer, the same step will be used for the **Title**, only this time instead of aligning the **Title** to the Right, you are going to align the **Title** in the **Center** as shown on (Image—O).

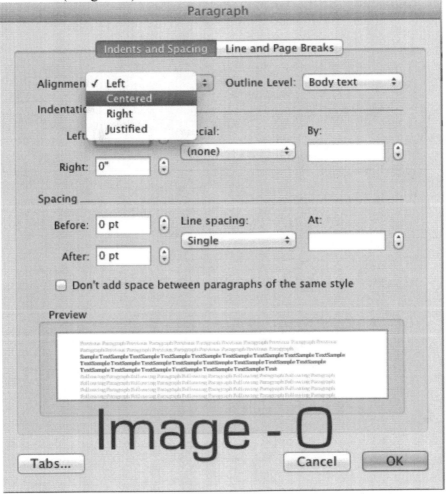

2. Now you are ready to Click **OK** and start typing your **Title**.

3. If you need a reminder on how to get to this screen just follow the instructions below:

   A. Go to the **Menu** and
   B. Click on **Format** and
   C. Choose **Paragraph**. Now that you have clicked on **Paragraph** (Image – N),

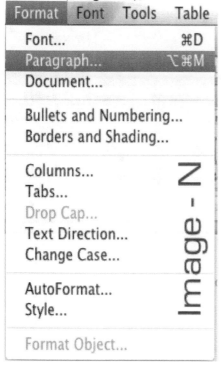

it opened up a new window where you can set the **Alignment** of your cursor (Image – O).

   D. Click on the **Left** button (it will open up a drop down menu where you can now adjust the alignment of the cursor to start on the **Left, Center, Right** of the paper (depending on what you want to do – as you are about to start typing the body of your paper, you should set it to **Left**. Now that you have selected the **Left**, click **OK**. Your alignment is now on the left hand side – Good work!))

*** Three Additional Notes When Titling Your Paper***

There are three things you want to keep in mind when you **Title** your paper. **First, you want to capitalize the start of every word in your Title with the exception of: articles** (a, an, the), prepositions (of, in, around, about, etc.), or coordinating conjunctions (for, and, nor, but, yet, so). The exception to this rule is that you do want to capitalize the first letter of the start of your Title, no matter of what it is. So, if the start of your Title begins with The, you want to capitalize the T (see Image – P).

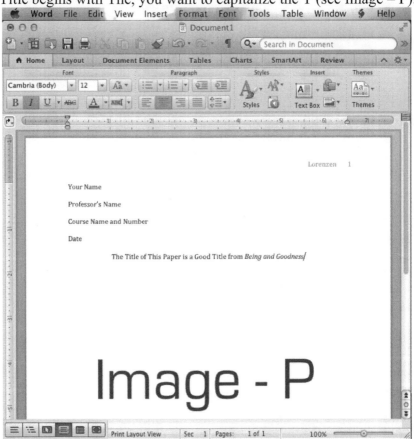

Second, do not capitalize a whole word or all of the words in your Title (See Image – P).

Third, you never underline your Title, but should you reference a longer/larger work *within* your Title, you need to italicize the book, magazine, or a longer/larger work. If you are referencing a relatively short work like an article for a newspaper or magazine or a poem then you will want to use quotation marks around the referenced work – just like you would in the body of your paper. If you take a look at Image – P you will see that I created a Title with a reference to a book within the Title. Notice how the book Title within the paper Title is italicized (See Image – P).

6. *The Content of your Paper: Formatting The Intro, Body, and Conclusion (MSWORD for MAC/Apple)*

You want to make sure that you have a double-space between your Title and the first line of your paper. If you look at Image – Q you will see that there is a double space between the Title and the first line of the paper, but if you keep reading the body of the paper, you will find that the rest of the lines are single spaced. I am going to show you how to double-space your paper. There are a couple ways to approach this: 1. You have already written your work and you need to double space. 2. You haven't started yet and you want to make sure every line is double-spaced. We are going to start with the first scenario first.

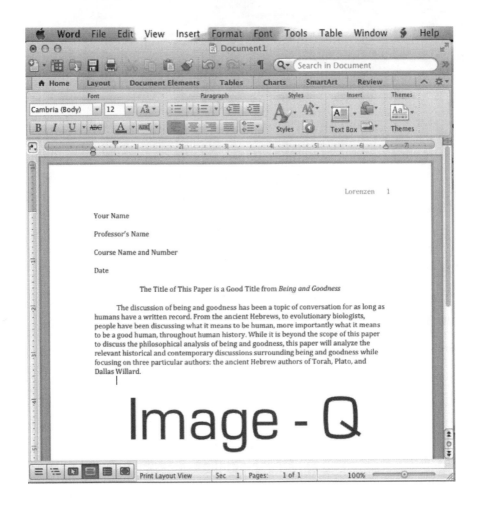

One Way (Way 1 - You have already writing your work and you need to double space your paper):

You have already written your paper or part of your paper and you need to make it double-spaced. The best way to do this is to select the text you want to double-space.

1. To do this, click on the word you want to start the double-spacing and move it throughout your paper to the last word you want double-spaced -- This will highlight all the words you want double-spaced (see Image – R).

2. As you can see from that image, after highlighting the text, you will now want to go to the **Menu** and select **Format** then select **Paragraph**.

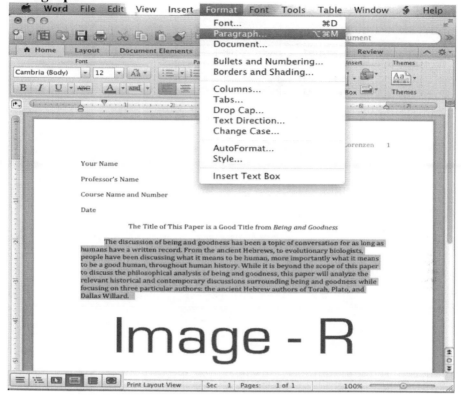

3. This will bring up a window with which you are familiar. Notice on (Image – S) that the **Line Spacing** box has been selected which gives us the option to **Double Space** our selected text.

4. Click on **Double**

5. Click on **OK**.

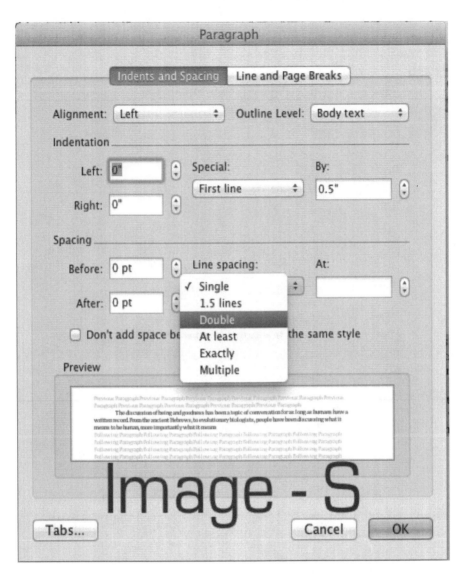

You can now see in Image – T that the selected text has been double-spaced and all text that is typed subsequently will be double-spaced as well.

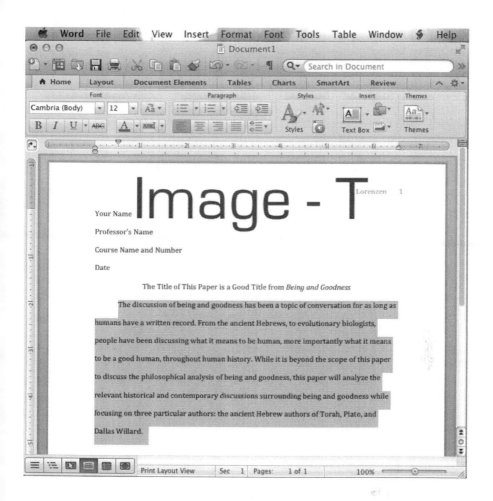

Other Way (Way 2 – You haven't yet started your work and you want to make sure every line is double spaced):

You are about to start writing your paper, but you need to make sure that your paper is formatted correctly.

1. You will want to go to your **Menu** and click on **Format**.

2. You will then want to click on **Paragraph** which will bring up a window with which you are familiar – see (Images - R and S).

3. You notice in the middle of the window that there is a selection for **Line Spacing**. If you click on this drop down you will notice that one of the selections is **Double** for Double spacing.

4. Select **Double**

5. Click **OK** (Image – S). You are now ready to start typing your double-spaced paper! **Reminder**: Always be sure to indent new paragraphs one-half inch (.5") for MLA standards.

Chapter 3: Formatting your Paper for – PAGES (by Apple)

Starting Your Paper (Pages):

When you start your paper your paper should look something like (Image - 1).

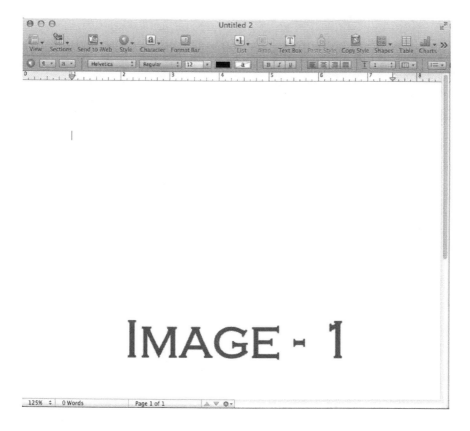

1. Paper Set-Up: Margins (Pages)

1. To set-up paper margins, use your **Inspector Menu** and click on the little image at the top of the **Inspector Menu** that looks like a blank piece of paper with the right hand corner ear-marked (Image - 2) (Do you see the one that is highlighted in blue with the red circle around it on (Image – 2)? This is the one you want to click on. For those of you with the

paperback version see (Image – 2) and the paper with the circle around it.)

IMAGE - 2

2. Once you click on this little paper image you will see that there is a section where you can change the Document Margins. The default selection is one inch (1") margins on the top and on the bottom, and for the left and the right. MLA guidelines state that the margins on all sides must be one inch (1"). This means that should your default be different than (1") you will need to change the margins on the Left and Right/ Top and Bottom to read (1") (Image - 3). (See the four circles on (Image – 3) below).

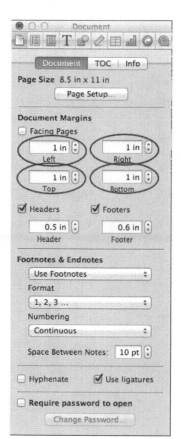

3. When you are finished typing in 1" margins on all sides you are now finished with your margins. Congratulations! If you need to adjust the margins for anything, just follow the same steps and adjust your margins accordingly.

2. Paper Set-Up (Pages): Header and Footer (Last Name and Page Number)

1. You might also have notices on the **Inspector Menu** that there are a couple of boxes for Header and Footer. Again, if your **Inspector Menu** is not showing up, just go back to the beginning of this section and follow the instructions on how to have your **Inspector Menu** show.

Unless you are instructed to do so by your professor, MLA guidelines do not demand a title page which means that it is best not to have one (unless you are told to do so – always check with your professor).

2. Make sure the boxes are checked for Headers and Footers. If they are not checked you will not have a Header or Footer in your document.

3. We are going to have to **adjust the alignment of the Header and Footer** before we get started.

A. To adjust the alignment click on the **T** (Text inspector) button on the Inspector Menu, see (Image - 4).

IMAGE - 4

B. This will bring up a new selection of choices, one of which will look like (Image - 5).

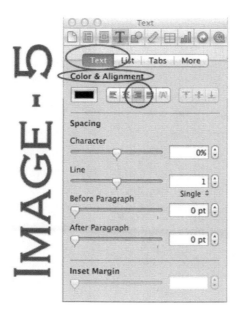

IMAGE - 5

C. Notice that Text is circled in Blue, and Color & Alignment is circled in Blue. Make sure that you have the **Text** button selected (see Image 4), at which time you will be able to see Color & Alignment.

4. You notice that one of the boxes is circled in red. This is a **Right Justify** Box. The box to the left of it is a **Center Justify** box, and the one to the left of that is the **Left Justify** Box (it is asking you where you want to start typing - from the Left, Center, or Right). Your Pages program is most likely defaulted to Left Justify, so you will need to **Right Justify** for your name. You are also going to have to add a Page number. Once you add the page number from this first page it will update every page thereafter with your Name and Page number on each page.

3. ***Inserting the Page Number***

An additional note to consider is that you can't just put in the number 1 after your name – Pages won't recognize that you are going to be counting pages after this first page.

1. So, in order to have Pages recognize that you are going to be counting pages after this page go back to your **Menu** and choose **Insert**.

2. It will bring down a drop menu where you will want to choose **Page Number**. You will notice that a page number appeared in the Header (Image - 6) (hopefully after your name,

45

assuming that you haven't clicked your cursor somewhere else).

3. If you look back to the **Margins** section of this manual, you will see that the Margins for the **Header and Footer** default to **.50/.60**or ½ inch. This is exactly where they need to be for MLA guidelines. If you find that they are off, just follow the instructions by going back to the **Inspector Menu** and adjust your margins to .50.

4. Also, always remember that your *Last name* and *page number* are flush against the Right side of the paper. When it is finished your paper should look something like (Image – 6). **Notice the last name followed by a space followed by the number 1, indicating that it is the first page of the paper.** You want to make sure that each additional page of the paper looks like this - except changing the number as the pages continue.

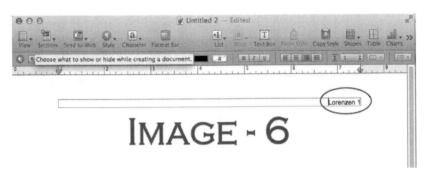

4. Paper Set-Up (Pages): Name, Professor, Course and Course Number, and Date

You are now ready to place your name, your professor's name, the course name and number, and date on your paper.

1. Starting from the top left hand side **of the body of your paper**, place your full name and double space; place your professors name and double space; place your course name and number and double space; and place the date and double space.

When you are finished your paper should look something like the picture in (Image -7).

5. Page Set-Up (Pages): Title of Paper

The next step is to place your title on your paper. You have just finished placing the date on your paper – you now want to double space after the date. If you remember back to the **Alignment** of the Header and Footer (**Inspector Menu →T→Text** (Color &Alignment)), the same step will be used for the **Title**, only this time instead of aligning the **Title** to the Right Justify, you are going to align the **Title** in the **Center Justify**, see (Image - 8, notice the Center Justify is circled now in red). Now you are ready start typing your **Title**.

47

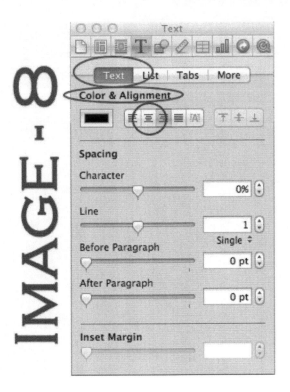

IMAGE - 8

*** Three Additional Notes When Titling Your Paper***

There are some things you want to keep in mind when you **Title** your paper. **First, you want to capitalize the start of every word in your Title with the exception of: articles** (a, an, the), prepositions (of, in, around, about, etc.), or coordinating conjunctions (for, and, nor, but, yet, so). The exception to this rule is that you do want to capitalize the first letter of the start of your Title, no matter of what it is. So, if the start of your Title begins with *The*, you want to capitalize the T (see Image – P - in the Word document section of this book).

Second, do not capitalize a whole word or all of the words in your Title (See Image – P in the MSWORD section of this book).

Third, you never underline your Title, but should you reference a longer/larger work *within* your Title, you need to italicize the book, magazine, or a longer/larger work. If you are referencing a relatively short work like an article for a newspaper or magazine or a poem then you will want to use quotation marks around the referenced work – just like you would in the body of your paper. If you take a look at Image – P you will see that I created a paper Title with a reference to a book within the paper Title. Notice how the book Title within the paper Title is capitalized and italicized. (See Image – P).

6. The Content of your Paper: Formatting The Intro, Body, and Conclusion

You want to make sure that you have a double-space between your Title and the first line of your paper. If you look at Image – Q (back in the MSWORD section) you will see that there is a double space between the Title and the first line of the paper, but if you keep reading the body of the paper, you will find that the rest of the lines are single spaced. **I am going to show you how to double-space your paper.** There are a couple ways to approach this: 1. You have already written your work and you need to double space. 2. You haven't started yet and you want to make sure every line is double-spaced. We are going to start with the One Way (Way 1) scenario first.

One Way (Way 1 – You have already written your work and you need to double space):

You have already written your paper or part of your paper and you need to make it double-spaced.

1. The best way to do this is to select the text you want to double-space. To do this, click on the word you want to start the double-spacing and while holding down the left mouse button move it throughout your paper to the last word you want double-spaced -- This will highlight all the words you want double-spaced. If you want to select ALL the text on your paper (which I don't recommend), a shortcut for this is Command-A (both pressed at the same time, it will select all the text). You will now want to go back to the **Inspector Menu→T→Text** (This should be familiar to you by now).

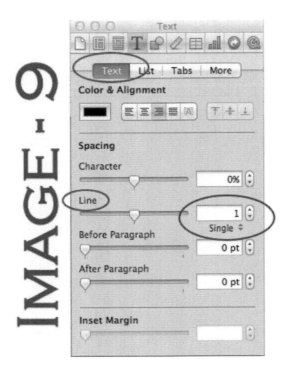

IMAGE - 9

2. If you take a look at Image-9 You notice that the **Text** button is selected with a blue circle around the **Line** button (for those of you with the paperback version it is the two circles on the left hand side of (Image – 9) and a red circle around the spacing. You have a choice here, you can either click on **Single** (see Single below the number 1) and change it to **Double**, or you can delete the number 1 and enter a 2. The choice is yours - either way it will double space your selected lines.

Other Way (Way 2 – You haven't yet started your work and you want to make sure every line is double spaced):

You are about to start writing your paper, but you need to make sure that your paper is formatted correctly.

1. Make sure that your cursor is double spaced from the Title of your paper, then follow the same steps as listed above to: **Inspector Menu→T→Text** (This should be familiar to you by now). Instead of double-spacing all of what you have written you are going to double space all of what you are about to write. **Reminder**: Always be sure to indent new paragraphs one-half inch (.5") for MLA standards.

Chapter 4: "The Fourteeners" - Style Suggestions

1. Always make sure to use 8.5x11 sheet of white paper for your assignment – unless otherwise instructed to do so.
2. You want the writing to be moving down the page lengthwise. If you are writing across the page 11 inches then your paper is oriented the wrong direction– unless otherwise instructed to do so. Follow the instructions on Images – U and V to change your page layout.
3. Paper Layout

How to "Layout" Your Paper Using MSWORD (for Microsoft)

If for some reason your paper is typing long ways across the paper (so that your paper is 11" across by 8.5" down) you will need to change the layout of the paper. To do so...

1. Click on the **Page Layout** button **on the Menu**.
2. Under the **Page Setup** section (towards the left hand side) there is a little box with a downward facing arrow in it. Click on that arrow (see MSW-15).

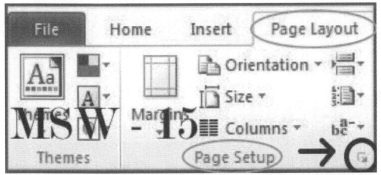

3. A new window opened up where you have the choice to change the **Orientation**. Make sure that the **Portrait** orientation is selected (see MSW-16)

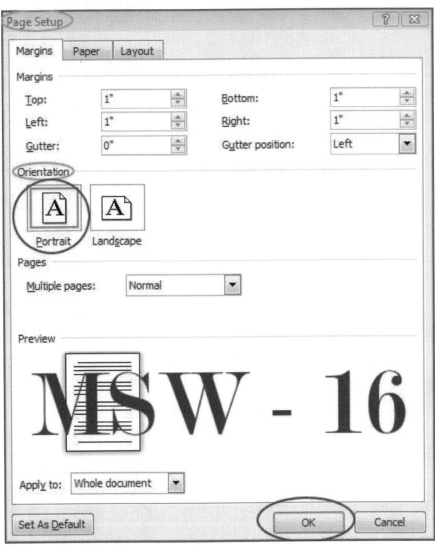

4. Click **OK** (see MSW-16).
5. Great! Now your paper is oriented the correct direction for MLA standards!

How to "Layout" Your Paper Using MSWORD (for MAC/Apple)

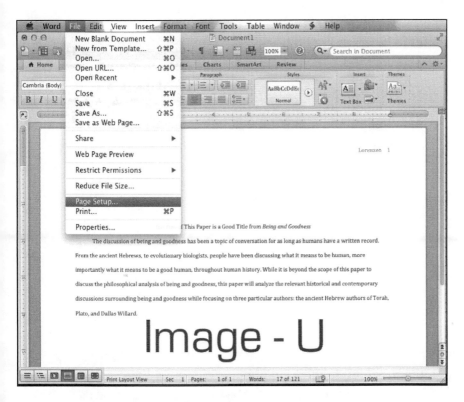

If you find your paper looking like that in Image – U, go to your **Menu** and click on **File**. Now go to the selection that says **Page Setup**. This will bring up a window that looks like Image – V.

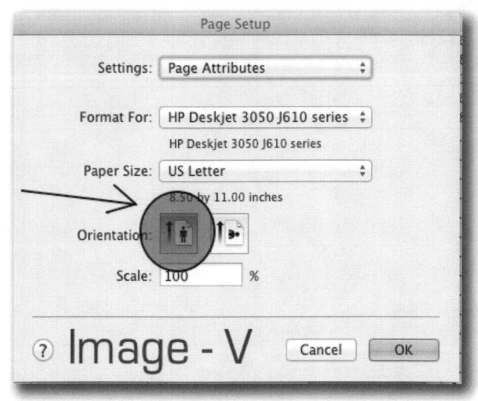

If you look at the middle of the window you notice that it says **Orientation**, with an arrow pointing at a man. You want the **orientation** to look like the man in the circle is standing up and down, not sleeping on his side like the other one. Click the box that shows the man standing up and down and click **OK**. Now your paper should look like the Images – A through T.

How to "Layout" Your Paper Using PAGES by APPLE

If you find that you need to change the layout of the paper (let's say that your paper is turned sideways so that the paper is now 8.5 inches top to bottom and 11 inches side to side) to do so go to your **Inspector Menu** (Image - 10)→**Document Inspector** (the little dog-eared white piece of paper in the upper left hand corner (Image 10)→**Page Setup...**(Image - 11)→**Orientation** (Image - 12)→**OK** (Image 12).

IMAGE - 10

IMAGE - 11

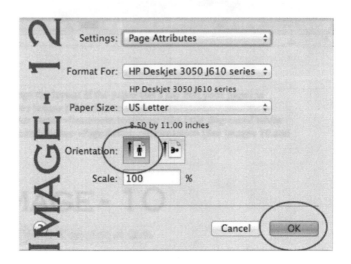

4. There are many acceptable font formats. One of the most common is Times New Roman, but there are many very readable fonts: Garamond, Arial, Roman, etc. The point is that you want your paper to be easy to read, so you want your font to be free from distractions – unless otherwise instructed to do so. As a college professor and K-12 teacher, there might be nothing as painful as reading 1000+ papers a year that all look alike – and when you get one that is hard to read because of a distracting font – LOOK OUT, student!

5. When you are learning to write in Kindergarten your teacher always tells you to put a finger space between your words so that they aren't too close together and aren't too far apart. When you are typing the same thing is necessary. As a general rule you only want a single space between an end mark (period, comma, semicolon, colon, dash, double dash, etc.) and the next word. There may be exceptions to this, but your professors will let you know if you are to make exceptions.

6. When you indent your paper, please make sure that you **DO NOT** use the spacebar to indent your paragraph – as this tends to mess up the formatting. Use the Tab button on your keyboard, as the Word document is programmed to indent the appropriate space by using the Tab button.

7. When you have set your **Line Spacing** to Double Space or **Double**, you only need to hit the enter or return button once when starting a new paragraph. Word has already been programmed to Double Space that next line when you hit enter or return.

8. Try to vary your sentences and paragraphs. If all your sentences sound similar then your professor will become tired of reading "just" another paper. Look at your paper as a piece of art that is compelling to look at.

9. A strong paper will have excellent transition sentences between paragraphs where the transfer between ideas is almost seamless. When you are moving onto another idea and you are going to start a new paragraph, try to lead into that idea at the end of the previous paragraph. Don't just jump into something new without already introducing it somewhere in the previous paragraph.

10. When you sit down to write a paper, take a moment to create a list of things you want to write about or include in your paper. The best thing to do is to try to brainstorm the things you want to write about and get them written down somewhere. It is not a bad idea to turn a blank piece of paper into a mess of writing all over the paper – you can always organize those thoughts later. For those of you that think something like that is insane, try creating an outline where you move sequentially through your thoughts where you discuss what you are going to write about and why you are going to write about it and your evidence for your presuppositions. The point is to organize and think before you write.

    a. Let me give you an example of how I teach some of my early writers to formulate their thoughts through outline:
        i. Paragraph 1 (Introduction to Essay)
            1. Introduce any ideas that your reader may need to understand your argument (your thesis sentence)
            2. State your thesis sentence(s)
        ii. Paragraph 2 (Body of Essay)

        1. Give a reason to support your thesis
        2. Give an explanation for your reason (include quotes, good reasoning, etc.)
        3. End your paragraph with a good conclusion to your reason while transitioning into the next paragraph and idea

  iii. Paragraph 3 (Body of Essay)
        1. Give a reason to support your thesis
        2. Give an explanation for your reason (include quotes, good reasoning, etc.)
        3. End your paragraph with a good conclusion to your reason while transitioning into the next paragraph and idea

  iv. Paragraph 4 (Body of Essay)
        1. Give a reason to support your thesis
        2. Give an explanation for your reason (include quotes, good reasoning, etc.)
        3. End your paragraph with a good conclusion to your reason while transitioning into the next paragraph

  v. Paragraph 5 (Conclusion)
        1. Revisit the big ideas/big reasons and how they fit into your thesis.
        2. **Whatever you do, don't introduce any new ideas/reasons into your conclusion.**

11. When I (Shawn) was studying literature and writing in my undergraduate studies, I rarely, if ever, revised my writing. My theory was "first draft-last draft." As I moved into my graduate studies, I quickly realized that my first draft was a

crap draft. As a result, I quickly learned to "tighten up" my writing and choose my words more carefully. While some of you might be able to get away with a "first draft – last draft," it is not a bad idea to get in the habit now of revising your work – at least look it over once.

12. Before your begin writing your paper **Start with your Works Cited page**. It is always easier to delete items than to add items, and you always have a handy reference on hand should you need an author's last name or something of the sort (just in case you took the book back to the library).

13. Visit your On-Campus Writing Center. They are paid good money to read papers – it is free for you, work for them, and another set of eyes looking over your paper for any errors or problems.

14. My last piece of advice for style is probably the most humbling; however, it has not only paid me huge dividends in my own studies, but also in my own writing—and that is to submit your work to at least two other people for review – people who are good writers. We write so many papers in college that we lose sight of the fact that we are submitting our work to someone else for judgment. I know that it hurts to have a peer look over and judge your work, but it will help you to become a better writer.

Chapter 5: General Grammar Concerns

Grammar Questions:

Grammar can be difficult to learn, especially if you have never been taught how to write. Below is an explanation of some of the most basic parts.

Parts of a Sentence:

Subject: *Who* or *what* is performing the action that the verb expresses or is having something predicated of it? The Subject of the sentence is NOT always a NOUN! **Don't** make the mistake of thinking that the subject is a noun.
Mark ran downtown. **I** am cold. **Running** is my favorite activity.

Predicate: This is the part of the sentence that comes after the subject – everything that comes after the subject is the predicate.
I **kicked the ball down the road**. Running down the street **is my favorite activity**.

Direct Object: (The verb must be transitive – needs an object to complete the meaning) Who or what is **receiving the action** of the verb?
He threw *the porcupine*. Mark kicked the **ball**. Marcie discovered **America**.

Subject Complement: Is there a linking verb or a form of "to be" followed by a noun or adjective that is "equal to" the subject?
Kinds of Subject Complements:
Predicate Nominative (Noun): Does it rename or identify the subject? (He is the ***president***. She became *a police officer*. It is *she*. Those are *they*. (Yes, the last two are proper grammar.) His name is **John**.)
Predicate Adjective: Does it describe the subject? (The dog was *blue*. The fish smelled *bad*.)

Prepositional Phrases: These function as either Adjectives or Adverbs.

Adjective example:

How much is that doggy *in the window*? (**Which** doggy? The doggy in the window).

Adverb example:

I put the paper bag *over my head*. (**Where** did I put the bag? Over my head.)

[*Every prepositional phrase must have an **object**. No object of a preposition is ever a subject or a direct object.*]

Indirect Object: To whom? For whom? To what? For what?
My grandpa built *me* a tree house.

Parts of Speech:

Noun: A noun is generally a person, place, thing, idea, or concept. Noun means name. Kinds of nouns: dog, concrete, beautiful, number, name.

Pronoun: A word that takes the place of a noun. There are different kinds of pronouns but the most common are I, you, he/she/it, we, you, they, etc. There are different kinds of pronouns: demonstrative, relative, personal, etc. The most important thing to remember about pronouns is that you always capitalize personal pronouns (Names): Susan, Mike, Statue of Liberty, California, etc.

Verb: What is *happening*, being done or performed? Is it an action? Is it expressed by a "to be" verb (*am, is, are, was, were, etc.*) or a linking verb (has, had, have, been)?
Mark **ran** downtown. I **am** cold.

Adverbs: Modify verbs and adjectives (they explain the verb or adjective in more detail). They answer the questions: Where, when, **how**, why, to what extent?
I am **very** cold. I **quickly found** the car.

Adjectives: Modify nouns (and possibly other adjectives). They (explain the noun or adjective in more detail) answer the questions: What kind? How many? Which one? Whose?
He kicked **the big** ball.

Prepositions: prepositions show relationships between things. For instance the preposition "between" shows a relationship between two objects: The chair is **between** the floor and the ceiling. I set the water bottle **on** the desk.

Interjections: Interjections interject statements or exclamations into sentences. **Oh**! I saw that movie.

Conjunctions: There are two types of conjunctions **Coordinating** and **Subordinating**. Coordinating conjunctions connect two independent sentences together. The FANBOYS are the Coordinating conjunctions: For And Or But Yet So. For example: I saw the bike. I biked home. I saw the bike, **and** I biked home. Notice how the two independent sentences became one sentence with the Coordinating conjunction (also notice how the comma separates the coordinated sentences. Whenever you have a coordinating conjunction join two independent sentences you will place a comma before the coordinating conjunction.
Subordinating conjunctions take an independent clause and join it with a dependent clause. Some subordinating conjunctions are: while, when, until, however, although. I went to the store (independent clause) when I rode my bike (dependent clause). Here the subordinating conjunction joins the two clauses.

Sentences: Every sentence must have a subject (actual or implied), a verb being or doing an action (either passive or active), and the sentence must have meaning or make sense – it needs to mean something to the reader. "Purple feels inside," is nonsense (non-sentence) because it doesn't communicate a thought or a feeling in someone else although it does have a subject and a verb.
Declarative sentences: Declarative sentences make a declaration. Example: I see a cat.
Interrogative sentences: Interrogative sentences ask a question. Example: Do you see a cat?
Exclamatory sentences: Exclamatory sentences make an exclamation of feeling or emotion. Example: That cat is awesome!
Imperative sentences: Imperative sentences make demands or commands: Example: Go find that cat.

Verbs as Voice (Active and Passive Voice): Your professor might tell you that you need to "avoid the passive voice." There are two kinds of **voice** for verbs: Active and Passive Voice.

Active Voice: Active voice is when the subject (of a sentence) is acting upon or doing an object. Example: Susie *hit* the car. The car *smashes* the light. Both of these sentences are in the active voice because the verb is showing that the subject(s) is acting upon or doing the object(s).

Passive Voice: The Passive voice occurs when the subject (of the sentence) is acted upon by the object. Example: The light *was smashed* by the car. The car *is hit* by Suzie. Both of these sentences are in the passive voice because the verb is showing that the subject(s) is being acted upon by the object.

Most professors will want you to use the active voice. Just ask yourself is the Subject of the sentence doing the action or receiving the action. If the subject is receiving the action from the object then it is passive, if it is doing the action then it is active.

PUNCTUATION (?.,:-;--!)

The Period: The End Mark that completes a thought. You use a period when you are done completing a statement that is a complete unit of thought.

The Question Mark: You use a (?) question mark to identify that you or the person writing the text is making an interrogative statement or question.

Mark said to Susan, "Did you steal my spinach cheese puffs?"

The Colon: No, this is not referring to the plugged up system in your body. This has a number of uses but it is often used to set off a list from a category.

The following animals will be on display at the zoo: Bears, Lions, Tigers, Mole Rat.

Notice there is an introductory phrase of "the following" preceding the list set off by the colon. This is generally a good formal writing practice.

THE PUNCTUATION RELATIONSHIP (I don't like you! Yes, you do!): The comma, semicolon, dash, and period.

When I explain punctuation to my grade-school students, I never teach them "rules" about punctuation. I try to help them see it functionally – as a relationship or parts to the whole in that the parts are functioning a certain way to make up the whole. To illustrate this, I usually hold up a piece of putty and compare the putty to a sentence. The putty is one unit, just like a sentence is one unit. As you begin to pull the putty apart the relationship between the putty in one hand begins to lose its relationship to the putty in the other hand. When you first start to pull on it, there is putty in each hand and it still looks like one big piece of putty but there is some distance between the putty in both hands which is still connected by a lot of putty (which makes it still look like one big unit). As you begin continue to pull the putty apart you see that the putty gets thinner and thinner between the two hands. In other words, while the putty still remains connected they are becoming more individualized units, until they become two distinct units (i.e two distinct sentences, or two different units of thought). I usually list them as follows:

Comma (the putty is in both hands and it has just begun to be stretched, and so it still looks like a big mass of relationship)

Semicolon (the putty is in both hands but the hands are further apart and the putty between the two hands looks like a rope connecting the two units of thought. The relationship between the two units is still strongly held together by the rope between them but it is not as strong as it was when it was a comma)

Dash (the putty is in both hands but the hands are even further apart and the putty between is beginning to look like Silly String or a noodle. The relationship between the two thoughts is there but they are really starting to take on more of their own identity: Sort of like Salmon and Trout (There is a relationship there but each one really has its own identity).

Double Dash (The silly putty is in both hands and widely stretched apart. The putty between hangs very thin and limp like that of a long hair stretched between the two thoughts. The thoughts are still connected but just barely. (The colon could be used like a double dash, as well)

Period (The silly putty in both hands are no longer connected together. Each one has its own unit of thought)

Now let us take a moment and compare the putty analogy to a sentence.

The Comma: The comma has many uses but I will mention the two most common. First, it separates a list of different items.

I want a bunch of beans, asparagus, milk, and hard boiled eggs.

Notice how the commas separate the different items.

Second, the comma begins the separation process of a thought in a sentence. This would be a separation where the two different units of thought are still very closely related to one another (sometimes it looks like the putty is still one big glob).

The Semicolon: This is what I call a "weak" break in a sentence. When you want to start a new thought but it is still somewhat attached to the old thought, and you aren't quite ready to end the old thought yet. The test for a semicolon is whether or not the words following the semicolon can "stand on their own" as a sentence - if they can, you need a semicolon.

I wish you would mind your manners; yet, it is pretty funny.

Notice how "it is pretty funny" is still connected to the original thought of minding manners (the glob of silly putty is no longer recognizable as each hand of glob is connected by a thick piece of silly putty in the middle of both hands).

The Dash - The dash is my favorite punctuation mark because of its many uses. I like to think of the primary use of a dash as a slightly stronger break than a semicolon yet weaker than a period. Sort of like a thin piece of Silly Putty barely holding two ends of two ideas together. One function of the dash can be similar to that of parentheses--setting off a phrase that is related to the main clause (or main idea), but could be omitted. In the preceding sentence, the clause following the dash (always constructed by typing two hyphens together) defines the function of parentheses; if the reading audience was very familiar with that function, the clause following the dash could be omitted; it is valuable information, yet it could be left out. Another function of the dash can be pure emphasis--setting off a word or phrase that may conclude a thought or bear highlighting apart from the rest of the sentence.

There is one conclusion from the evidence of the crime scene--murder.

Exclamation Point - The exclamation point is used to exclaim something! It is overused today as a means of expressing surprise or excitement over trivial issues (Hello!); rather, it is intended to exclaim something that really is to be exclaimed - The argument was never intended to begin a war!

Period – The period completes a unit of thought. (There is no connection between the two distinct pieces of silly putty. They are now two individual units of thought.

(The Paragraph: If you think of the analogy in terms of sentences and paragraphs, the analogy holds true for these, as well. The sentences within a paragraph should have a common thread, they should all be held together like a piece of silly putty that is beginning to be split apart is still held together by some stringy silly putty in the middle. It isn't until we make a new paragraph that we break that thread holding the two ends together. Each one is now its own individual unit of thought.)

Spelling: One of the worst mistakes a student can make in this wonderful technological era is to fail to run a spell check over their paper. Depending on the size of the paper and the quality of one's spelling, it can take anywhere from 2 seconds to five minutes – and yet, if one doesn't do this, it can be the difference between an A paper and an F paper. Please take the time to run a spell check over your paper.

We are going to show you how to run a spell check using Microsoft Word and Pages by Apple. Lets Start with Microsoft Word

1. Spell Check for MSWORD(for Apple or MAC)

Go to your **MENU→TOOLS→SPELLING AND GRAMMAR**. You will notice that if something is mfspelled, it will not only underline that misspelling in red (within the document itself), but it will also recognize it in the spell checker and mark it as red in the spell checker, see the image below.

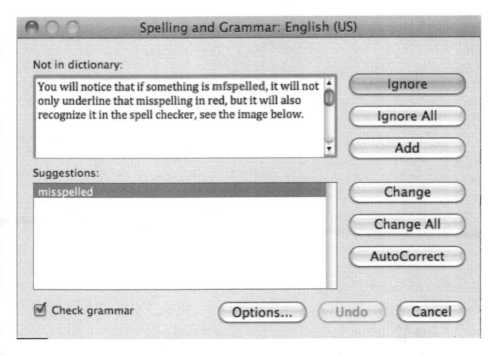

Notice how you have several options: Ignore, Ignore All, Add, Change, Change All, AutoCorrect, Options, Cancel. Let me take a moment to explain what each of these will do.

Ignore: If you click Ignore, it will ignore only this misspelling that is spelled "mfspelled."

Ignore All: If you click Ignore All, it will ignore every misspelling that is spelled "mfspelled."

Add: If you click Add, it will add the word to the Dictionary, so that every time you write that word, it will recognize it as an actual English word. The word "Lorenzen" is not recognized in the dictionary, so when it comes to the word "Lorenzen" I always add my name to the dictionary so that I don't have to correct it every time.

Change: If you click on Change, it will change this word marked in red to the word that is highlighted in the "Suggestions:" box (See the image above). In this case, I would click Change because I want to change this word from "mfspelled" to "misspelled."

Change All: If I click on Change All, it will change every words in the paper that is spelled "mfspelled" to "misspelled."

Auto Correct: If I click on AutoCorrect, it will change EVERY word in the paper that is misspelled to the first suggestion in the "Suggestions:" box.

Check Grammar: If you want MSWORD to correct or check your grammar for you, then you can click on "Check Grammar."

Cancel: If you don't want the Spelling Grammar tool to do anything then click "Cancel."

2. Spell Check for PAGES by Apple

Go to your **MENU→TOOLS→SPELLING→SPELLING**. You will notice that if something is "msspelled," it will not only underline that misspelling in red (within the document itself), but it will also recognize it in the spell checker and mark it as red in the spell checker, see the image below.

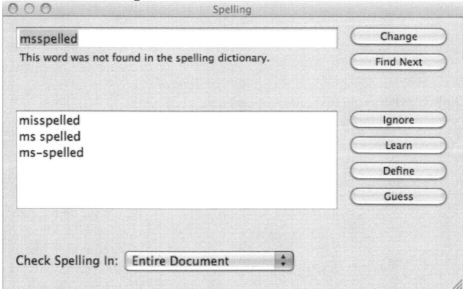

Notice how you have several options: Ignore, Change, Find Next, Learn, Define, Guess. Let me take a moment to explain what each of these will do.

Ignore: If you click Ignore, it will ignore only this misspelling that is spelled "msspelled."

Change: If you click on Change, it will change this word marked in red to the word that is first listed in the box below the misspelled word (See the image above). In this case, I would want to click Change because I want to change this word from "msspelled" to "misspelled." If you want to choose a different word other than the first suggested word, just click on it with your cursor and it will choose that spelling.

Guess: If I click on Guess, it will change the word in the paper that is misspelled to the first suggestion in the "Suggestions:" box.

Find Next: If you click on Find Next, it will go to the next misspelled word on your paper, and it will NOT correct this misspelled word.

Learn: If you click on Learn it will pass-over the word and will not mark it as a misspelled word. It will not add it to the Dictionary, but it will not mark it as misspelled any longer within your document.

Define: If you click on Define, it will tell you the meaning of the word.

Spell Check for MSWORD (for Windows)

1. Go to your **Menu** and click **Review** (see MSW-17).
2. On the Left hand side you will see a big check mark with the words **Spelling & Grammar** below it. Click on this **big check mark** (see MSW-17).

3. It will bring up a couple of different boxes depending on if there is a grammar mistake or a spelling mistake. The next step will guide you through the different choices of your mistakes.

4. **Grammar Mistakes** you will have several options (see MSW-18).

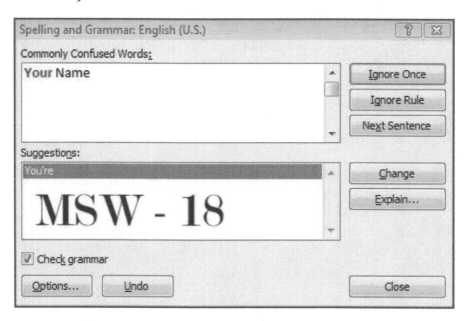

Ignore Once: If you click Ignore Once, it will ignore only this grammar mistake once, but it will ask you about the others.

Ignore Rule: If you click Ignore Rule, it will ignore the grammar rule that is being applied.

Next Sentence: If you click next sentence, it will check the grammar in the next sentence.

Change: If you click on Change, it will change this word marked in green to the word that is highlighted in the "Suggestions:" box (See the image above). I would not want to do this in this case.

Explain: If you want it explained, then click Explain.

Close: If you don't want the Spelling/Grammar tool to do anything, then click "Close."

5. **Spelling Mistakes** will also have several options (see MSW-19).

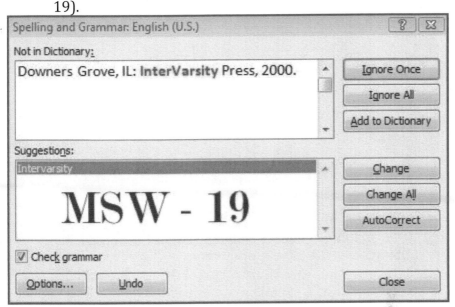

Ignore One: If you click Ignore Once, it will ignore only this misspelling or questionable misspelling.

Ignore All: If you click Ignore All, it will ignore every misspelling that is misspelled or questionably misspelled.

Add to Dictionary: If you click Add, it will add the word to the Dictionary, so that every time you write that word, it will recognize it as an actual English word. The word "Lorenzen" is not recognized in the dictionary, so when it comes to the word "Lorenzen" I always add my name to the dictionary so that I don't have to correct it every time.

Change: If you click on Change, it will change this word marked in red to the word that is highlighted in the "Suggestions:" box (See the image above). In this case, I would not want to change it since it is the title of a publishing company

Change All: If I click on Change All, it will change every words in the paper that is spelled incorrectly, to the word in the "Suggestions" box.

Auto Correct: If I click on AutoCorrect, it will change EVERY word in the paper that is misspelled to the first suggestion in the "Suggestions:" box.

Cancel: If you don't want the Spelling Grammar tool to do anything then click "Cancel."

"Other Marks"

Quotation Marks: Quotation marks go around words that are quotes. Example: The author said, "The problem of individuation is a problem of properties."
Notice: Notice that the quotes go around the first word quoted and the end mark (in this case the end mark is a period). Always make sure that the quotes go **after** the end mark.
Notice: Notice that there is a comma before the quote and the quotation marks. If you are starting a quote in the middle of a sentence, make sure that you put a comma before the quotation mark.

Parentheses: Parentheses are for parenthetical statements. For Example: I saw the man (not just any man, a weird man) standing at the front door delivering milk. Notice how the parentheses give a little bit more information, in this case about the man, within the sentence, but the information really doesn't have anything to do with the sentence. Also, parentheses can just be something else said within the sentence. Example: Cheeses (they make me pass gas) that are filled with hormones and other foreign substances are found in certain kinds of milk cows.

Brackets: Brackets are used to include words, phrases or clauses which are used to explain the words or clauses that proceed them. Example: I forgot the philosophical problems [the problem of individuation, the qualia problem] which resulted in me failing the test.

Chapter 6: Paper Guidelines

1. Is your first page formatted properly?
2. Do you have a clear **thesis**?
3. Do you provide **supporting information** that relates to your thesis? Is it relevant? Be sure to use quotes, paraphrases, and summaries well. Include **page numbers, author** and the correct **format:**
Quotes:
"...the beginning of my ultimate demise" (Smith 231).
Paraphrases/Summaries:
...he recognizes his hopeless situation (Johnson 52).
4. Is your paper well **organized**? Is there an intentional and logical relationship between each part of your paper?
5. Do you use a consistent and formal **tone** without lapsing into colloquialisms?
6. Is your **sentence structure** correct and appropriately varied?
7. Did you use correct **punctuation** and **capitalization**?
8. Is your **spelling** accurate and your **vocabulary** effective and colorful?
9. Does your writing and formatting display acceptable **neatness** and readability?

Other Considerations:

-Are you creative in your presentation of the material?
-Do you fulfill what the thesis statement promises?
-Have you made sure you did not include any irrelevant or insignificant information?
-Did you make sure you did not plagiarize?
-Did you have someone else proofread your paper?

Chapter 7: Formatting Citations within the Body of Your Paper

Books, Journal Articles, Newspapers, and Magazines: When **quoting** from any of the previously listed sources you will want to follow a couple of key guidelines.

1. You will always want your source quoted to appear in the **Works Cited** page in the appropriate order (we shall discuss in greater detail the **Works Cited** page later on). If you take a look at Image – W, you notice that Dallas Willard is the first quotation in the paper, but his book will be the last full reference on the **Works Cited** page <u>because entries are listed alphabetically by author's last name</u>.

When examining the good life and what it means to be a good person, one of

the most natural areas to start is in the area of epistemology – can I know whether

or not I am, or someone is, a good person? Dallas Willard argues that we have

knowledge of something when it is accurately represented "on an appropriate basis

of thought and experience" (15). This idea of representation and alignment with

reality doesn't seem to be too distant from Plato's view of knowledge. In his work,

The Meno, Plato (by means of the mouth of Socrates) seems to argue that knowledge

is something akin to an atrium of birds or a swarm of bees and you don't really

know something until you *grasp* one of the bees or birds (15). This notion of

grasping something has strong connotations of intentionality and commitment to

having it. For the Hebrew culture, much of their discussion involved a way of life

where "the fear of God is the beginning of knowledge" (*The New American Standard

Version Bible*, Proverbs 1.7). All three of these sources indicate that there is a way of

knowledge that is not merely propositional in nature but require other

2. The way the reference is entered into your paper depends on how you quoted the individual in your paper.

a. If you take a look at image (W) you notice that Dallas Willard is introduced earlier in the sentence as the person making the argument; this means that his name does not appear in the referenced parenthetical at the end of the sentence, even though there is a direct quote at the end of the sentence.

b. If you take a look at the next referenced sentence you notice that Plato is referenced without a quote (a paraphrase), and because his name is referenced earlier in the sentence as the author, his name doesn't appear in the reference at the end of the sentence. Again, you only have the page number.

c. If you look at the third referenced source you notice that it is a Biblical reference which is treated a little differently. (If you encounter a situation where you are quoting an ancient text like the Bible, see the full MLA Handbook for further details. This is not a common occurrence, and most biblical references would be handled in writings of theology, which generally use Turabian formatting instead of MLA.)

Now let's take a closer look at each of these three examples:

The Direct Quote (<u>with</u> Author referenced in the sentence)

Sentence 1 (Direct Quote): Dallas Willard argues that we have knowledge of something when it is accurately represented "on an appropriate basis of thought and experience" (15).

Explanation: When the Author is quoted within the sentence you **don't** need to include the author within the parentheses. You only need to include the page number. **Notice: The quotation marks end, then you have the page number in parentheses, then you have the end mark (in this case, a period). The quotation marks will never contain the parenthetical reference (Author pg#).**

The Paraphrased Idea (with Author referenced in the sentence)

Sentence 2 (Paraphrased idea): In his work, "The Meno," Plato (by means of the mouth of Socrates) seems to argue that knowledge is something akin to an atrium of birds or a swarm of bees and you don't really know something until you *grasp* one of the bees or birds (15).

Explanation: Here the idea of Plato is paraphrased and the paper is giving credit to Plato for coming up with the idea. Because Plato is mentioned as the author of the idea within the sentence, his name doesn't need to be included in the parentheses.. **Notice: The ending with the (15). The end mark always follows the end parentheses.**

The Unknown Author Citation

Sentence 3 (Biblical Citation): This notion of grasping something has strong connotations of intentionality and commitment to *having* it. For the Hebrew culture, much of their discussion involved a way of life where "the fear of God is the beginning of knowledge" (*The New American Standard Version Bible*, Proverbs 1.7)

Explanation: There are as many different *kinds* of Bibles as there are different kinds of cars. When quoting the Bible there **is no given author and it is a longer work** but there is a given *kind* of Bible. You notice that the *kind* of Bible (New American Standard) is not mentioned in the sentence but there is a quote given from the Bible. In this case the *kind* of Bible is referenced in the parentheses in *italics* followed by the *book* (Proverbs) of the Bible followed by the chapter and verse. **Notice: 1. The kind of Bible is in italics, and there is a comma separating the kind of Bible and the book of the Bible. 2. There is a period separating the chapter and verse.**

Shorter Work with Unknown author: The Bible is a long work but if you are quoting a shorter work with an unknown author you need to place the work in parentheses with quotes around the title of the work follows by the page number like this: ("The Known Way" 5).

Direct Quote (<u>without</u> the author referenced in the Sentence)

Sentence 4: All three of these sources indicate that there is a way of knowledge that is not merely propositional in nature but require other dispositions or categories such as belief. A belief is a "map or view of the world, what he holds to be true about it" (Swinburne 122).

Explanation: You notice in the book reference that the author is not mentioned in the sentence, and yet the author is quoted. This means that you need to reference the author's last name followed by the page number. **Notice: There is no comma or period between the author's last name and the page number.**

The Paraphrased Idea (<u>without</u> the author referenced in the Sentence)

Sentence 2 (Paraphrased idea): Knowledge is something akin to an atrium of birds or a swarm of bees and you don't really know something until you *grasp* one of the bees or birds (Plato 15).

Explanation: Here the idea of Plato is paraphrased and the paper is giving credit to Plato for coming up with the idea. Because Plato is not mentioned as the author of the idea within the sentence, his name does need to be included in the parentheses. **Notice: The ending with the (Plato 15). The end mark always follows the end parentheses.**

Multiple Authors

Sentence 5: While the debate over properties and substances is difficult and arduous to work through, Moreland and Rae simply state that "properties have owners, and a substance owns properties" (70).

Explanation: When dealing with multiple authors you treat the in-text citation the same as a single author. In this case the authors are mentioned in the sentence; so, only the page number is needed within the parentheses. Should the authors not be mentioned within the sentence their last names would need to be referenced in the parentheses like this (Moreland and Rae 70).

One Author in a Series

Sentence 6: The Categorical Imperative of Kant is all brakes and no gas which begins with the idea that, "We all act according to what Kant calls maxims" (Copleston 6: 320).

Explanation: There are two parts to this explanation: 1. If there are several quotes from several different volumes in the same series then you want to address the reference as I did above (Author's Last name Volume Number: Page Number) **Notice that I included the author's last name because the author was not mentioned in the sentence, otherwise the reference would look like: (Volume Number: page number(s)).** 2. If there is only one book out of the series that you are referencing in your paper then you only need to include the page number: (320) – unless of course you didn't mention the author in your sentence in which case it would look like this (Copleston 320).

Internet Source – Direct Quote

Sentence 7: Knowledge then can be defined as "the capacity to represent a respective subject matter as it is, on an appropriate basis of thought and/or experience" (Willard, "Knowledge and Naturalism").

Explanation: Electronic sources are tricky, but there are a couple of things you can do as a "rule of thumb." If possible, include the information (author's last name, title, etc.) within the sentence. If the author and/or title is not referenced in the sentence then you want to direct the reader to the right spot on the works cited page. In this case, the author is listed first followed by the work. **Notice: There are no page numbers.** Internet sources, most of the time, do not have page numbers. In this case the author and title is not referenced in the sentence so it is given within the parentheses and that is all that is needed for this reference.

Internet Source – Paraphrased

Sentence 8: The capacity to represent something as it is on the appropriate basis of knowledge and experience is often something discussed in Willard's writings such as *Knowledge and Naturalism*.

Explanation: If we are going to paraphrase something by an author then we need to include the best way to lead the reader to the works cited page. In this case we listed the Author's last name within the sentence as well as the article that was paraphrased. **Notice: There is no parenthetical reference on this internet source.**

Chapter 8: Tables and Graphs (the short chapter)

The general rule for tables and graphs is to keep them as close to the reference(s) as possible. This might require a little bit more work from your computer and knowing the computer program. From my experience in writing one dissertation, editing one dissertation, and writing hundreds of papers over the past 25 years, I have found that it is better to use an "insert" button rather than a "cut-and-paste" method. The insert button allows you more flexibility and the computer seems to understand what it means (even though it doesn't understand anything).

Chapter 9: Formatting the Works-Cited Page (for Windows)

Your Paper should already be formatted for Double Spacing. If it is not just go back to the section on **Page Set-Up: Name, Professor, Course, Course Number, and Date for MSWORD (Windows)**

With that said, there are some changes you need to make to your works cited Page.

1. Make sure that you start your Works Cited Page on its own Page (don't just start a Works Cited page in the middle of a page right after you finished typing your paper – your Works Cited page needs its own page(s).
2. Make sure that your Works Cited page is titled with **Works Cited**.
3. Make sure that **Works Cited is centered** in the middle of the page - To do so, go to your **Home Menu**.
4. Find the **Paragraph** section. And click on the button for **Center** (see MSW-13).

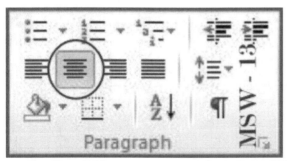

5. Great! You are now ready to type Works Cited for your paper! **Type Works Cited!**
6. When you finish typing Works Cited, **hit enter or return** (on the keyboard).
7. You will notice that the cursor is still in the middle of the page. We need to align that cursor to the left-hand side of the page. To do so go to the **Home** Menu (again, you should already be here). Find the **Paragraph** section in the middle of the Home Menu. Click on the **Left Align** button (see MSW-12).

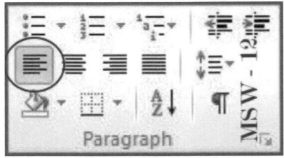

8. You are now ready to start typing your entries in the Works Cited portion of your paper!

9. However, before your start typing your entries there are a couple of adjustments we need to make to your settings. Got to your **Menu** and click on the **Page Layout** Button.

10. Find the **Paragraph** section in the middle of the Page Layout menu. On the bottom right hand corner of the Paragraph section you will see a little box with an arrow in the middle of it (pointing downwards). Click on that arrow.

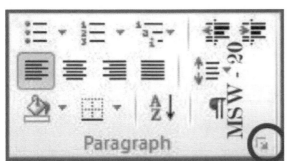

11. It will bring up a new window entitled Paragraph. You will need to make sure that the **Left and Right** Indentations both say **0"** (see MSW-21).

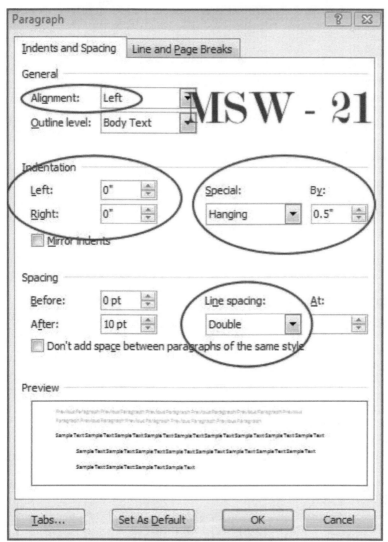

12. You will also need to make sure that under "Special" that **Hanging** is selected (see MSW-21).

13. In the box that says **By:** (right next to the Hanging box)make sure that it says **0.50"** in that box (see MSW-21).

14. Also, it is good to double check that your **Alignment is Left** (see MSW-21).

15. Double check that your **Line Spacing is Double** (see MSW-21)

16. Click **OK**. Great Job! MLA format requires that for any Works Cited page, that if an entry goes over one line in length that

every line of that entry that follows is indented 0.50"; as a result, your entries should look something like image MSW-22.

17. You are now ready to start typing your Works Cited Entries.

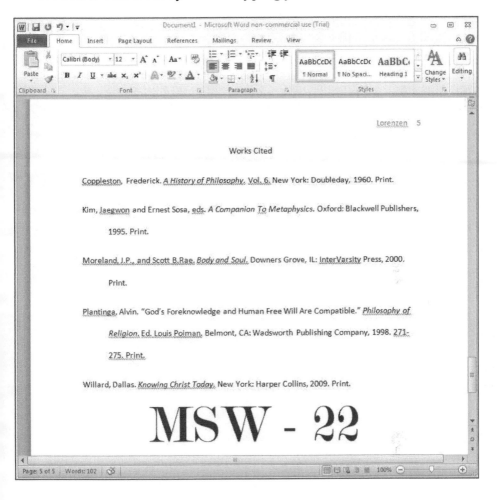

Chapter 10: Formatting the Works Cited Page with MS WORD (for MAC/Apple)

Works Cited

Lets start by taking a look at five examples on a works cited page (Image – X).

Works Cited

Copleston, Frederick. *A History of Philosophy.* Vol. 6. New York: Doubleday, 1960. Print.

Kim, Jaegwon, and Ernest Sosa, eds. *A Companion to Metaphysics.* Oxford: Blackwell

> Publishers, 1995. Print.

Moreland, J. P., and Scott B. Rae. *Body and Soul.* Downers Grove, IL: InterVarsity Press,

> 2000. Print.

Plantinga, Alvin. "God's Foreknowledge and Human Free Will Are Compatible." *Philosophy*

> *of Religion.* Ed. Louis P. Pojman. Belmont, CA: Wadsworth Publishing Company,

> 1998. 271-275. Print.

Willard, Dallas. *Knowing Christ Today.* New York: Harper Collins, 2009. Print.

Image - X

Seven Quick Steps to Formatting the Works Cited Page

1. You want format your Works Cited page the same way you formatted your paper. As it will be the last page(s) of your paper, you will want to make sure that your Works Cited page is listing the right page number and your name in the upper right hand corner of the paper.

Next, you will want to make sure that the title "Works Cited" (see top of (Image – X)) is one inch (1") from the top of the page (since you have already defaulted your paper to start 1" from the top of the page, this shouldn't be an issue. If it is, just follow your formatting steps that were shown to you earlier in this book to format the page.).

2. You will **Double Space** between the "Works Cited" title and the first entry – see (Image-X).

3. **One Inch Margins** – Just like the rest of your paper, your "Works Cited" page will have one-inch margins on each side.

4. Double Space between entries. You see that the first entry only takes one line, but the second entry takes two lines. Please make sure that you **Double Space** between entries.

5. Double Space between lines on the same entry. You see that the second, third, and fourth entries all have "hanging" entries which take up another line on the paper. That next line must be double-spaced.

6. ½ Inch Indent on "hanging" entry(ies) – you notice that the second, third, and fourth entries have that entry that bleeds or moves onto the next line. This next line and every other line that follows **on the same entry** need to be indented ½ inch. Let me show you a few steps to make this work easily for you:

Step 1: Take a look at (Image – Y) and notice how the second, third, and fourth entries are not indented like (Image –X). Make sure that your cursor is on the entry you want to "fix" by indenting or highlight your whole entry. You need to go to the **Menu** and click **Format** and click on **Paragraph** (see Image – Y).

Step 2: It brings up that familiar formatting box that you know so well. Now if you look at (Image – Z) you notice that you click on **Special** and click on **Hanging** .

Image - Z

Step 3: Next to hanging you will see a white box that says "By:" – In this box you will want to write 0.5" (it may come up automatically, as the computer generally defaults to this setting) see (Image – AA).

Image - AA

Step 4: Click **OK**. Now your entry should look something like the ones on (Image – X). Repeat the process at many times as necessary for "hanging" entries.

7. **Alphabetical Order** - If you take a look at (Image – X) you notice that the entries are listed in alphabetical order. You must list your works in alphabetical order starting with **Author's last name** as seen on (Image – X).

Chapter 11: Formatting Works Cited Page with PAGES by Apple

Formatting your Works Cited Page in Pages is really easy.

1. Go to your **Inspector Menu** (Image - 13)→**T** (Text inspector, Image - 13)→**Tabs** (Image 14)→ First Line or **Left** (Image - 14 Depending on what you want to do).

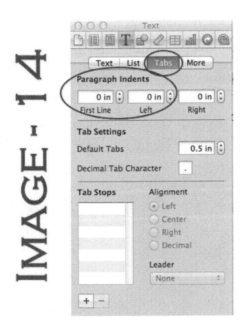

Let me take a moment to explain what is happening with Image-14 and why I circled both the First Line and the Left. When you are working with Works Cited you are usually going to be working with a couple of lines. If you only have one line then you don't have to do anything. However, when you have multiple lines then you are going to have to do something with the second line (remember: all Works Cited entries must be double-spaced). If you have more than one line you DO NOT want to do anything with that First Line entry in Image -14. What this is telling you is whether or not you want to indent the first line of your paragraph - We don't want to indent the first line of any of our Works Cited entries because it is not MLA. However, we do want to indent the other lines after the first line to .50.

So you would go the line that needs to be indented, click your cursor on the beginning of that line (the far left-hand side of the page), then go to the box that says **Left** and enter in **.50 or click on the up arrow next to the box** a couple of times until it says **.50**. That second line will now be indented to .50 which is MLA standard. If you have a third or a fourth or a fifth line, go ahead and repeat the step each time for each line.

Remember, you need to do this for each Work Cited entry that has more than one line.

Chapter 12: Works Cited Page

The following examples are some of the more common situations you will encounter in your research. If you find yourself needing to cite something beyond the scope of this book, please reference the MLA Handbook.

When dealing with titles of books and articles, use the same capitalization rules that we discussed earlier, in the section regarding the title of your paper.

One quick tip on titles within the Works Cited Page: As a general rule, *Italicize* all titles except if the titles are a work within a larger group of works like: poems, an article within a journal, a web page within a web page, a chapter of a book, a short story, etc.

All of the titles that come from a work within a larger work will all have quotations around the title.

Book: One Author (Image – BB)

Remember to double space within and between all Works Cited entries. Do not underline the period following the title of the book.

Citation Style:

Author's last name, Author's first name. *Title of Book*. City of publisher:

Publishing company, year of publication. Print.

Willard, Dallas. *Knowing Christ Today*. New York: Harper Collins, 2009. Print.

Image - BB

Notice: The word PRINT at the end of the citation. For any non-periodical print publication you need to put the word "Print" after the year of publication.

Book: Two or More Authors (Image – CC)

List the first author with his/her last name, then first name. Subsequent authors are listed in order they are listed on title page, with their first name first. For more than three authors, list first author (Last, First), then et al.

Citation Style:

First author's last name, First author's first name, and Subsequent author's

First and Last name. *Title of Book.* City of publisher: Publishing

company, year of publication. Print.

Moreland, J. P., and Scott B. Rae. *Body and Soul.* Downers Grove, IL: InterVarsity Press,

2000. Print. Image - CC

Book: Edited Book (Image –DD)

In an edited book, the emphasis could be either the work of the primary author or the work of the editor. For example, a book of Edgar Allen Poe selections chosen by an editor focuses on Poe; a book of compilations concerning a unifying subject by many different authors would be an example of a book that focuses on the editor, since they did the work to compile the work of various authors. Notice in the example below, with two editors, that the same rule applies as to two or three authors.

Citation Style:

Editor's last name, Editor's first name, ed. *Title of Book.* City of

publication: Publishing company, Year of publication. Print.

Kim, Jaegwon, and Ernest Sosa, eds. *A Companion to Metaphysics.* Oxford: Blackwell

Publishers, 1995. Print. Image - DD

Book: Selection from Anthology (Image – EE)

Provide in the Works Cited the page numbers for the entire essay/work to which you refer, regardless of the number of citations in the paper.

Citation Style:

Author of essay's last name, Author of essay's first name. "Title of

Essay."

Title of Anthology. Editor of anthology's first and last name. City

of publication: Publishing company, Year of publication. Page

numbers of essay. Print.

Plantinga, Alvin. "God's Foreknowledge and Human Free Will Are Compatible." *Philosophy*

of Religion. Ed. Louis P. Pojman, Belmont, CA: Wadsworth Publishing Company,

1998. 271-275. Print.   **Image - EE**

Book: Multi-Volume Work (Image – FF)

If the volume you are using has an individual title, cite without
mentioning the other volumes; when the volumes have the same title,
include the number of the volume you are using.

Citation Style:

Author's last name, Author's first name. *Title of Volume*. Volume number.

City of publication: Publishing company, Year of publication.

Print.

Copleston, Frederick. *A History of Philosophy*. Vol. 6. New York: Doubleday, 1960. Print.

Image - FF

Book: Scholarly Edition (Classical Literature) (Image – GG)

If an editor is mentioned in conjunction with a particular piece of
classical literature that you are using, it most likely indicates that they
have been involved in choosing from various versions or translations to
present it to the reader with certain choices made in regards to language,
spelling, etc. This editor should be recognized in the citation.

In the example below, we are referring to a particular work of
Plato's in his complete collected works. Include that title, as well as page
numbers, as you would in a selection from an anthology; if these situations
do not apply to you in citing the work of classical literature that you are
using in your research, do not include them.

Citation Style:

Author's last name, Author's first name. *Title of Work.* Ed. [abbreviation

for editor] Editor's first name Editor's last name. City of

publication: Publishing company, Year of publication. Print.

Plato. "Theaetetus." *Plato Complete Works.* Ed. John M. Cooper. Indianapolis: Hacket, 1997.

157-234. Print.

Image - GG

Journal: Scholarly Journal (Image – HH)

Remember that the author you are citing in conjunction with a journal is the author of the article, not an editor of the journal. Following the title of the journal may be a few variations of relevant information, like issue numbers, volume numbers, series numbers, etc. Cite whatever is provided. For example, cite the issue number alone, if there is no volume number provided. Cite both volume and issue numbers if both are included. If a series number is included, cite that as well. The example below (Image – HH) contains a series number. If a journal designates that a series is a new and original series, indicate this with ns or os before the volume number

Citation Style:

Author's last name, Author's first name. "Title of Article." *Title of*

Journal # of series [abbreviated ser.] [if applicable] Volume.Issue

number (Year of publication): Page numbers. Print.

DeWeese, Garrett. "Timeless God, Tenseless Time." *Philosophia Christi* 2ⁿᵈ ser. 2.1 (2000):

53-59. Print.

Image - HH

Magazine: Article from a Magazine (Image – II)

Magazines differ from journals in their citation in one key way—do not cite volume and issue numbers for a magazine, even if they are cited printed on the issue. Cite only the date—full date (day, month, year), or month(s), and year. For full date, use day month year format, abbreviating all months except May, June, and July.

Citation Style:

Author's last name, Author's first name. "Title of Article." *Title of*

Magazine Date Year: Page numbers. Print.

Oakes, Edward T. "Philosophy in an Old Key." *First Things* Dec. 2000: 27-34. Print.

Image - II

Web Source that is not "in print;" its only source is on the Web:

Let's be honest, most of our information is going to come through the Web these days. So, it is important for us to know how to cite a work that comes from the Web. Here are a few things to keep in mind when quoting or citing from a Web source. First, you want to cite all the information that is available in this order:

1. Author, editor, translator, compiler, etc. (whoever is responsible for getting the work on the web-site).

2. Title of the work (it needs to be italicized unless the work is part of a larger work (or group of works), in which case, use quotation marks around the title).

3. Web Site Title (if different from Work Title).

4. Version or Edition.

5. Publisher (if the site has a publisher, if no publisher write *N.p.*).

6. Date of Publication (as much as is available).

7. Medium of the publication (in this case it is the Web).

8. The day you accessed the website (when you actually found your source material).

(9). MLA does not require a URL (which is genius because they are always changing and people do searches instead of typing in a particular URL). However, should you decide to include a URL make sure to set it off with brackets like these: <> or to give an example: <www.dallaswillard.com>

Let us take a moment to show you how this might look for us: Let's say that we are looking up phenomenology the Stanford Encyclopedia of Philosophy web site and we come to the site show below in (Image – KK).

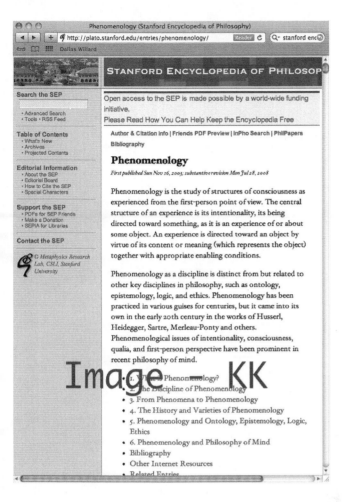

In this case the Work Cited entry would look something like this (see below and Image – LL):

Author. *Title*. Web Site Title. Publisher. Date of Publication. Medium of

Publication. Date of Access.

Smith, David Woodruff. *Phenomenology*. Stanford Encyclopedia of

Philosophy, 2008. Web. 01 Sept. 2012.

Image - LL

The most important thing to keep in mind when citing any Web page in your Works Cited Page is to include all of the relevant information in the appropriate order according to MLA standards.

Web Source that also has an "in print" version (Web version of books, journals, periodicals, oh my!):

The difference between the "**non**-in print" and the "in print" source is that the "in print" source is a book, journal or periodical that you might be able to check out from the library or buy from a bookstore, but you can also read it on the Web. One of the most popular ways this happens today is with Google Scholar. With Google Scholar you can read books that have been scanned into a website, which are available to be read by anyone and everyone. (If you haven't used this site I highly recommend it for scholarly work – just do a search for Google Scholar, and you will find a Google Website devoted to searching through scholarly journals, books, and periodicals.)

For every work that you access on the Web that has a corresponding print text or has been scanned from a book, you want to treat the citation as a regular print citation with the following exceptions:

1. Instead of writing Print at the end of your citation, the medium or publication is Web – so you write Web at the end of your citation, instead of Print.
2. You want to include the Title of the database or Website (make sure this is Italicized in your citation).
3. Include the DAY you accessed the information in the following order: (day, month, Year,)
4. You can include a URL, but again, it is not necessary.

96

You may include as much information as you like, just make sure it is accurate and in the correct order **according to the Print guidelines for Works cited.**

Works Cited: Final Look

I just wanted us to take a final look at a Works Cited Page and remind us of some of the "big picture" things to keep in mind (see Image – JJ).

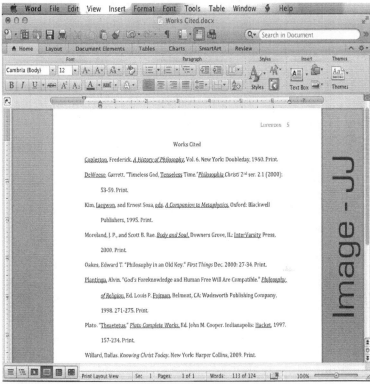

Notice:

1. All entries are double spaced between each other.
2. All entries are double spaced in and of themselves.
3. All entries are in alphabetical order according to the first word entered in the work cited.
4. All entries say **Print,** because they are all Print texts.
5. All entries where there is more than one line are indented (1/2 inch or .5) after the first line (hanging indent).
6. Last name and page number are in the upper right-hand corner.

7. Works Cited page is recognized on the first line and centered in the middle of the page.

Chapter 13: Wrapping-Up

As I said at the beginning of this book, there is a fully developed book (by the gurus of MLA) at your local library waiting to equip you with all of the nuances of MLA standards and guidelines. While this book was intended to give you a good starting point regarding formatting by means of Word and Pages, it is by no means exhaustive. If you believe that there is something that needs to be added to this book, which will add to the "starting point" aspect of formatting a paper for MLA, please don't hesitate to let me know at lefthandedwritings@gmail.com or www.lefthandedwritings.com. Or if you have any other comments, I would love to hear from you and dialogue with you. Thanks for using this book, and happy MLAing!

Made in the USA
San Bernardino, CA
21 March 2014